T0094829

day/break

day/break

Gwen Benaway

Book*hug Press
Toronto 2020

FIRST EDITION

copyright © 2020 by Gwen Benaway

ALL RIGHTS RESERVED

No part of this publication may be reproduced or transmitted in any form or by any means, electronic or mechanical, including photocopying, recording, or any information storage or retrieval system, without permission in writing from the publisher.

LIBRARY AND ARCHIVES CANADA CATALOGUING IN PUBLICATION

Title: Day/break / Gwen Benaway.
Other titles: Daybreak
Names: Benaway, Gwen, 1987– author.
Description: Poems
Identifiers: Canadiana (print) 20200158929 | Canadiana (ebook) 20200158988
ISBN 9781771665735 (softcover) | ISBN 9781771665742 (HTML)
ISBN 9781771665759 (PDF) | ISBN 9781771665766 (Kindle)
Classification: LCC PS8603.E5561 D39 2020 | DDC C811/.6—dc23

PRINTED IN CANADA

The production of this book was made possible through the generous assistance of the Canada Council for the Arts and the Ontario Arts Council. Book*hug Press also acknowledges the support of the Government of Canada through the Canada Book Fund and the Government of Ontario through the Ontario Book Publishing Tax Credit and the Ontario Book Fund.

Canada Council for the Arts | Conseil des Arts du Canada

ONTARIO ARTS COUNCIL
CONSEIL DES ARTS DE L'ONTARIO
an Ontario government agency
un organisme du gouvernement de l'Ontario

Funded by the Government of Canada | Financé par le gouvernement du Canada | Canada

ONTARIO CREATES | ONTARIO CRÉATIF

Book*hug Press acknowledges that the land on which we operate is the traditional territory of many nations, including the Mississaugas of the Credit, the Anishnabeg, the Chippewa, the Haudenosaunee and the Wendat peoples. We recognize the enduring presence of many diverse First Nations, Inuit and Métis peoples and are grateful for the opportunity to meet and work on this territory.

Cover photo by Filip Mroz (via Unsplash)
Interior cover photo by Syed Ahmed (via Unsplash)

"If I'm transformed by language, I am often
crouched in footnote or blazing in title.
Where in the body do I begin."

—Layli Long Soldier, *Whereas*

trans women are objects we must perform the gender of our bodies beaten to death by men in viral videos on Facebook a crowd mocks a trans woman in Paris then chases her down a street before punching her a man stabs his trans girlfriend more than forty times in the front seat of his car in a parking lot at 2 am my best friend texts me that she wants to die and I and I and I and I and and I

don't know how to stay alive

I refuse I refuse I refuse I refuse I make light I refuse I refuse I refuse I offer up my body I refuse I refuse I refuse I refuse I live I refuse I refuse I refuse I refuse I imagine elsewhere I refuse I refuse I refuse I refuse I refuse I withhold I refuse I refuse I refuse I refuse I refuse I persist I refuse I reuse I refuse

I

am not

an object

I inscribe my gender like a bruise on the perfect smooth flesh of

your bright morning

the dawn (and I)

begin as colour across the horizon, granulated and coarse, not

ordered or linear, submerged in light and dark

incorrigible diffuse daybreak

I confess my beauty

then you murder it.

1

I am not a girl
but a creature made of smoke
and exhaustion.

I want a poem scrubbed of
dignity,
a body
not brave
but present.

once
after fucking me hard
in a bedroom filled with dust,

you said I was more or less
like a biological woman.

I carry your words inside my body
like the night carries the moon—

each time I wake,
less of me is left.

still, the low sounds
of the city rise up
to wash my hands clean
of longing

my morning cigarette
is a prayer
to mourn
the end of sleep.

look to your own horizon

tell me what you see.

is it my breasts,
wet with your saliva,
returning to press
against memory

or does nothing of me remain?

I asked for this, didn't I?

to be in love
and not broken,

luminous,
suspended in air.

brief light
of this new day,

bless us
in our forgetting.

2

a tranny is a girl
who sold her dignity
for a chance
to be human.

I am the lesser woman,
transformed by scalpel
and the indifference of men.

their careful pity
marks my body,
the border
between want
and shame.

call me hunger
and place your flesh
on my lips.

I want a gender
that does more
than perform apology.

I break bread
on the shoreline
and offer my throat
to the crows.

dip your hands

in my wet
and dive, lover.

I'm here,
a mistake
as much as envy.

3

the summer we met
I was 5'7 and 130 pounds,

all thirst and hunger but rail thin,
my hip bones jutting
out of pale skin.

you poured me over
your body,

musk stung
and glistening.

before you,
I knew nothing of how deep
abjection

could wound me.

now I've layered fat over
the places you touched
and held my fingers
against my labia

as if pressing a knife cut
shut.

please say my name
between the hours of dawn
and nightfall.

each consonant
will be a moth

in flight, circling
what light lingers.

rape is such
a small word
to hold what passed
between you and me.

I want you
to remember

that summer heat,
the roiling night clouds,
hum of insect and passerby,

my mouth
against your neck,

the dull wet sound
my body made
beneath you.

4

a poem
or a transsexual is never

made or unmade

by our descriptions,

the chromosomal
line breaks.

I would rather be a trick of metaphor
than a phantom of everyday failure.

how my body
conjures the ugly ruined world,

my blemished skin,
imperfect pitch.

there's a limit
to language—

each morning
the sun sweeps across the glass
towers in my city,
breaks into a million vessels
of flicker and blaze.

no one talks about
the ordinary wonder
of daybreak
though we wait for its arrival.

it's the same with a woman
or a girl—
not worth praising,
beyond words.

this is what the poem
and a transsexual want,

to be past
what can never be said
in proper speech,

to remain,
inviolate and brazen,

in the margins
of the sky.

5

I remember the weight
of your arm
slung over my shoulders
as we walked down
Yonge Street.

the yoke of your body,
how you parted seas of people
and muddied light to pull me

behind you.

loving a white man is

to be a passenger
in the wake
of his wanting.

6

did I ever tell you about the other boy?

I must have.

he was your opposite,

gentle and withdrawn,
refused to touch me
with anything
but grace.

his body
came between us
in conversation,

I wanted your jealousy to rise
and drown me.

I never gave him a chance
to love me,

determined
to have your hate
fill me full

of oceanic sediment.

I let him kiss me
in a rented car
in scarborough,
his hands of night
and aftershave.

how much I failed

by not imagining more
from love,

accepting someone's fetish
as my price,

playing queer in the absence
of any other name for what it means
to fuck a girl
like me.

7

to write of wanting,
to say "trans,"
meaning more
than identity,

lay claim
to this body
of pleasure
and skyline,

to be undone
by the scent of tree pollen
in a man's hair,
how the damp skin
of his lower back
could be a field
of yellow hay,

to admit failure,
the imperfect lust
of a woman
with no right
to call herself
female.

to linger in the shallows of love,
its oxbow curve
and glacial drainage,

to be sentimental
without justification,

praise the hymns
of city noon,
make elegies of
fast-food wrappers,

to conjure stretch marks
and body hair,

bear the weight of too much wanting
without the defence of beauty

or hope.

8

why remember
the tiny details,

your Minnesota accent,
your brown beard
against my cheek,
the bruises
on my thighs
from your grip.

when what I want now
is beyond proof,
more than confession
or memorialization.

I wear my body like the lake
wears the shore,

rubbed at, worn away,
eroded to a thin blue.

I wake in what the archive can't contain,
sleep in the mattress imprint
of your body next to mine.
call love what it is—

a worship of
the hereafter,

the bits left over,

scraps,
your laugh,
the sour smell
of your sweat,

my hands
against your back,
searching for an opening.

9

forgive me
my refusal to celebrate
your cock
and how you tore me
open.

I will not lay the riverbank's bright grasses
underneath your feet
to ease the passing
of what's already over.

I am what you made me,
every day I tire
of performance
and apology.

at least now I know
what happens between a man and woman.

you kill me
over and over
until my body
is a ruin.

10

I overdose on oxycontin,
eight small white pills.

slip down
into total
numbness.

I wake up the next morning

still alive,
still in love with him.

even my suicide is unrequited.

he texts to ask how I'm doing.
I tell him the truth:

lol I'm not great tried to kill myself last night

he calls me six times in a row.

I wait two hours
before calling him back.

his voice wavers on the line,
furious, terrified.

he asks
is someone with you

but doesn't offer
to be with me.

I hear the noise of cars rush past
through the phone's speaker.

no I'm alone I just don't want to live like this
anymore

streetcars rumble by
his heavy breath.

he keeps saying

I love you tremendously you are a woman you've always been a woman

please

11

I practise undressing in front of you, unbutton my jeans
unhook my bra kneel
in the slanted afternoon light, open my mouth,

wait for you.

I ask you not to call me
good girl

it creeps me out.

you tell me

it's healing though. like yeah daddy, I'm your good girl and I want to please you

push your cock into my throat
as far back as possible,
buck your hips.

I imagine

your body a concrete pillar
sunk into a river.

I break around you,
slick over
the roughness
of your pubic hair,

you whisper
good girl
to the rhythm
of your thrusts.
I choke on saliva and cum,
breathe through my nose,
count backwards in my head
until it's over.

I don't feel healed but wonder

what's wrong with me

when will I
be good?

12

he wore his body like a boy pretending to be a man. rode a red
bicycle down bloor street to meet me. denim jackets, second-
hand clothes he stole from goodwill. we eat cheeseburgers in bad
diners across toronto, fight in public parks and on the subway. I
fall asleep on his shoulder in an airplane en route to vancouver.
his hand rests on my leg as if I am a wild deer, lured close to him
by the scent of salt.

why is love ordinary and cruel?

everything I remember of him could belong to any woman who
fell in love with any man in this city.

loving him made me feel as if I were a part of the world. the riot
of new leaves in may breaking open above us. each cluster of
stars above the danforth, sudden and sharp as if I forgot that light
could travel between galaxies and reach us. winter in kensington
market, thin coats and his broad chest breaking the wind in
front of me. dry heaving when he left me, suicidal emails and the
infinite collapse of my hoping.

of course, it's cliché.

men blame women for feeling hurt by how things end but excuse
themselves for never being brave. I want to crawl through time
and grab him by the shoulders, shake him and shout

look at me

13

use the words

nothing
something
somewhere else

to float my body
down the river's grey tongue

populate the poem
with images I stole
from my life

a boy bends his arms down
laces his fingers together
lifts me up into a tree
around me
cherry blossoms fall
not beautiful
but ruinous

something moves between
the boy and me
haunting with gardenias
down every pathway

look, there's my mother weeping
over my missing genitals

my father, dead at last
by cancer and old age

my face ages
even as my tits grow bigger
all this nothing
is a creek in my heart
wetness in the inner values

say somewhere else
imagine a robin's beak
pecks apart my skull
miniscule cracks
in everything's filament.

14

he told me a story
of his grandmother's farm
in Jamaica,
something about goats
and the way sunlight scolded
every moment.

I was too distracted
by his beauty
to listen.

I couldn't buy his love with my body
though I tried again and again
to fuck my way to
liberation.

I want
to be desired

by what's forgotten.

for him to remember
my hair falling
across his face,

the wound
caught in my mouth.

how memory ruptures us
whole again,
in pieces
and too late.

15

I said my name to the nurse
and confirmed my date of birth.

she put a needle in my spine,
then I felt nothing.

when I woke up, I was past something—

he brochure they gave me when I left
didn't tell me what.

almost a year later
I make eye contact with a boy

who once said he just wanted to take care of me,
then didn't.

an ocean roars between his eyes and mine.

I understand the price I paid
for the sweet ache between
my thighs.

I write "post op trans girl" in my dating profiles.

I pretend my body is a body
redeemable.

somewhere someone wants what I have,
but what I have

is a handful of lake water,
a dead sparrow at dawn.

maybe what I'm past isn't my body
but my future.

16

there's beauty
in everything that breaks open.

a robin's egg,
the sun in summer,
a girl beneath a boy,
a tranny
in a hospital bed.

each wound
another chance

to birth light.

17

a birth certificate is a poem
the government
writes for you.

I've changed my name
my sex
my gender

still
this fraudulent country calls me
"sir."

18

how many times do I recount
the ways
my body was cut,
peeled apart and sutured
in anesthetized slumber,
for you to hear me?

it didn't make me a woman.
I'll never be so
precious.

I have a mouth
between my legs
that speaks the estuaries
of river and dusk.

I would do it again,
even
with a doctor's disdain.

the bloody mucus between my fingers,
my cries while someone
whispers *faggot*
to an orderly.

surgery wasn't about fixing my sex.

I wanted to make
a gesture,

a tear in the lining of me,
a scar where

day could enter.

19

should I give details?

for months
I lay on my back
watching blood flow from my vagina
like mud from a stream.

each day
I counted sutures as they dissolved,
revealing what surgery
had bought me.

my lover came to visit once.

my best friend called to say
it was too much for her.

I went to three emergency waiting rooms
only to be thrown out at dawn,

called a liar
and a whore.

shot full of morphine
and regret,

I almost died
in a hallway.

I watched my body, drugged on whisky
and oxycontin,

lie in his bed
as he described the cis girl
he fucked the night before,

stood naked in the shower,
trembling on legs
that could not stand without buckling,

and cried into the warmth of water.

now I perform the pitiful tranny

eager to say
what is wanted,

how well I'm trained.

I write about the girl who can't be loved
without being
murdered.

no language I have
can ever show

what it feels like

to touch
my clit

hard and hurt
like a marigold stem,

wet as a
sturgeon's
mouth.

my pleasure,
a secret language

to refuse meaning.

20

a tranny's mouth
is a vulgar hole

delusion's reservoir.

the health clinic's diagnosis

patient presents with
persistent gender dysphoria

pushes my body
toward the horizon
called "woman"

I never get to the peninsula
where the sun touches
the shore

no one closes their arms
around me
says
welcome home

I thought
faith acts on premonition
but since

I walked through the hospital doors
sat on the operating table

I stop waiting
on miracles.

the truth is

everyone's gender was
built on my disappearance.

21

a trans girl fills the inner eye of any camera,
excess is her garden.

I am here,
blossom in your annex bedroom,
pond and moonlight.

you got into photography
to document your conquests.

cis girls in sepia tones,
their bodies draped over furniture,
your shadow on their skin.

I've watch them appear on your Instagram
like wildflowers in alleyways,
unlooked for and precarious
as if they might disappear
in your camera,
never seen again.
it's my turn
to be visible,
no longer the ghost beneath you,
secret vice made
flesh.

you promised to photograph me
after my surgery,
witness my becoming
in celluloid sheets,
document how
I escape definition.

it doesn't feel like I imagined,

my breasts posed in the dark of your bedroom,
an empty house,
your mouth fixed in a careful line,
a half erection hidden
in your jeans.
every click of the camera
reminds me

I'm so far away
from beautiful.

I read an essay by another trans girl.

she said desire was not looking at the object
but imagining the looker in relation to the object.

you arrange me,

your lens like your dick
finds the right angles
to get you off,
makes me
into less than a girl,
more than a body.

to look is a kind of love.
it imagines the object in relation
to the subject.
that relation
is called *need*,

but you forget

the camera doesn't see the body,
only the energy around the body.

not the lips, but the gloss of lips.
not the girl, but her taste against the air.
not me naked in your bedroom,
but the moon behind me.

not your fingers on the shutter release,
but the sound of your tongue
against my spine.

once you said I wasn't a woman,
just "asserting the identity of a woman,"

mistaking the body for its image,
the relation for the object,
the aperture for the truth.

when I left you,
the last thing I did
was open your camera,
expose the film

to light.

22

the heart bends back on itself
into ontologies without English names.

I touch your shoulder
with the spine of a book
ask if we can talk.

you shake your head
as if I were your child
asking you
for candy
in a grocery store line
too poor
to answer with anything
but an unvoiced no.

the poverty of our youth
was more than economic.
I never learned how to love
without first asking
how much does it cost?

I stare into the wound
behind your eyes.
there's a history
to your hurt
your body a diaspora
I can't put my arms around

your mouth an island
I won't ever visit.

our love is impossible

the optics of our skin
the weight of our fathers.

you learned to not show emotion in public

because white people mark your body as
dangerous
in need of
containment or killing.

I'm sorry
I didn't see you
until I saw the shape of your absence.

I stand empty-handed
in the watching room
before you.

there's nothing to say

except

I love you

I'm here

in this body
meet me
halfway
in the pain

of two lives
we don't have words for.

23

between my legs
my body opens to forever

name me by the softness of your touch

look for a sound that catches
in my throat before
midnight spills around us

two scars cup my labia
wet them to draw out
the ache of birth

speak now or never say my name again

there is a low place inside me
the blue dusk
over your tongue

graceless, I break
under you

say starlight say moon
say I am the night
emptying from your body

here we labour with possibility
I am weary with the hunger
we unmake ourselves with

you will fall apart at dawn

but for a moment
you are whole above me

and nothing needs burning

here I am the deepest pink

the lining of a salmon's belly
a peony crushed underfoot

I flower with tightness
flinch away from the movement
of your body in mine

here the interior of my body
meets the world

this is as deep as you can
touch me
without killing me

when the light finds your eyes in mine

our bodies make their own logic
birth a politic
neither hopeful nor deceitful

not male or female
only animal

this breath I draw through my lips
pulls you into waters

blessed with salt
and the voices of dead women

repeat the words
goldenrod lilac and violet
until my skin is coated in pollen

everything becomes empty

first
the field fills
with
my
body

you must cross over me
to reach the other side
of her

say now
say yes

say you were only waiting
for me to unfurl a canopy of birches

the promise of my sex
is not in your mouth
wet and rising

but in my laugh

the sudden breath carrying
the heat
of our bodies

we will not say love
knowing enough

of grief
to speak

truer words.

24

weary of holding your heart

your disappearing
of me
meets the Vancouver skyline

a violent encounter
we call love.

I wipe rain from
my face, feel stubble
in my upper lip

it feels like I will never be warm again.

you repeat it will be ok
over and over
I play along to ease you off my back
keep you from breaking
my skin open again.

am I the abuser or the abused
you the hero or the foil

or are we neither?
two bodies
caught in an intimacy

that contracts and expands
like a heart.

I listen to your breath
asleep by my arm

question our love

like a wren builds a nest
piece by piece carried

in a thin beak, plucked
from an infinite blue cold.

I wake up in the early morning
stumble outside to smoke

return to our room

jar you awake
by the sound of the door closing.

you cry out "hello"
in a child's voice

and I answer

"don't worry, babe. it's just me."

you are sometimes helpless
and it makes me forget the ways you hurt me.

once you raped me
though we don't use

that hard word

we say "because of our history"
or "what happened in your apartment"

I was new on hormones
my breasts budding

you had me undress
cradle them for you

press them together
then you squeezed them

your eyes wide, hungry
I felt my stomach drop.

I want to defend you
I didn't say "stop"

just whimpered, bit my lip

later you say you liked
crossing my boundaries
then claim

I made you fuck me
and you didn't want me

but I washed the blood away.

the tear inside me
left a scar.

in Vancouver, the rape
is everywhere around us

I press my face into your chest

let you rub my back
imagine a safety
I don't feel.

once you admitted you abuse me
then we never spoke about it again

it's easier
to avoid the memory
when I'm not locked in a room
with you for days.

I'm sorry
I thought the trip would be romantic

and it is
you take me to the ocean
to watch the sunset

with a bottle of whisky tucked
in your value village coat.

you cry by the shoreline
I sit away from you

on the rocks
as light disappears.

you hold my hand
ask me in your voice

"you're cold, aren't you?"
and I am, I'm colder than

lake superior.

you take my picture
look at it

and say "damn, girl"
as if I was beautiful.

I wish you had lifted me up
in your arms toward

the darkened sky
and thrown me into the ocean
held me under

until I escaped you

called me pineshi
let me fly

with wings dipped in the rust of
oil tankers

away from you
and back to myself.

you didn't.

you loved me

and that was worse
though I won't admit it

until later.

25

why is it never enough
to say "I loved you"
and be done with it?

do you remember
sitting with me in a tim hortons?
your hands in mine,

you said I could meet your mother
and visit minneapolis.

I did everything you asked of me

wore makeup
got the surgery
trained my voice
grew breasts
practised sweetness
between your legs.

now all we are
is a poem
I wrote from the ruin
of our bodies.

"Sometimes a body is that which happens to you"

—Billy-Ray Belcourt, "NDN Homopoetics"

26

there's always sunlight in new orleans

my hands never seem to dry
caught in yours
our bodies descend
through the ninth ward
drunk on gin
and daybreak
your laugh
like a house
collects and holds
every possible joy.

you're the first girl
I've ever kissed
with tongue

and that slow pressure
of your hands between my thighs

mixes with the sound of a rooster
crowing next door.

all day, people walk past your front porch
and say "hello"

as if we're all familiar

you chain-smoke american spirits
wear crop tops that show too much cleavage
clear polyurethane heels

here and there
the city swelters closer
I ask you
if it's possible
for a trans girl
to ever be loved

you laugh
blow smoke in my face

lean in
to kiss me.

27

some nights
we sit in the bathtub together
smoking, drinking tequila

my body between
your legs

my back against your chest
wondering if

this much intimacy
is safe.

you pour water
from a plastic cup

over my neck, run your hands
down to cup my breasts

before kissing
the curve of my spine.

this is a loving
more deliberate
than I know
how to handle.

you make a joke
about my new vagina

say "if you still had a dick
we wouldn't be doing this"

and I pretend to laugh
as if it's funny that I've bled my way here.

later when my mouth lowers
to your clit

you gasp above me
and I wonder if we taste
the same now

haunted by the casual way
you remember the difference between our bodies

how I've come into
this wanting flesh

by force.

after you cum
and fall asleep beside me
your arms hooked around my waist

I slip away
to lie in the living room.

alone in a new orleans night
my head swims
with water.

28

you take me to climb railcars at dusk
abandoned beside the mississippi

there's a row of empty lots
one dilapidated house
surrendering to rot
a lone restaurant marks the end of the road
music plays
and a woman sings old jazz standards

her voice bathes the air
in longing

we brought beer
cigarettes
our empty bodies

half drunk
you tell me
the vacant lots
and the ruined house
are an old plantation

don't look over there
too long

in new orleans
nothing lets go
things linger
and they will follow us home
if you let them

so I don't look
caught by your eyes
in the slow turn of nightfall

each singular trace of your arm
against mine

your mouth, its incandescent taste
of flint and ash

we keep watch over the river
as the restaurant's singer
breathes out a mediocre cover of "feeling good"

of course
there's a haunting between us
the plantation's afterlife fills
the space behind us

still your hand in mine
makes another music

and we are
brief as the air in
your lungs
momentarily
here

I will not pretend
we can shed histories
like the city resists
the pull of hurricanes
and erosion

imagine your body
next to mine is a breakwater
a levee
against all hurts

to refuse joy
is the braver act
the only choice
girls like us

have left.

29

we fucked the same guy
for two years

some nights he came from me
to you
our bodies overlapping
through his

you say
queer love is fucking your ex's ex

I'm not convinced
we can flatten our desires

into anything as easy to name

without first killing

what makes us
human.

30

a boy fucks you
while I wait in the other room
listening to the slap
of his body against yours.

we talked about having a threesome
but I'm glad we didn't.

I've seen too much of men
to let a stranger fuck me
while you watch.

the ceiling fan sends
currents of cigarette smoke
out the open front door into the street.

a car passes.
someone calls out hello
to the driver.

you cum
a shuttered gasp
that bends the day
back on itself.

I don't envy him
your pleasure.

afterwards you come into the living room
take the cigarette from my fingers
kiss my mouth, still wet
with him

ask me what I want to eat for lunch.

we go uptown for oysters
you walk between him and me
take turns holding hands.

we follow you
caught in something
as sudden

as rain.

31

new orleans is
the only place I've ever been
where time staggers home
drunk.

though everywhere I find
evidence of history's neglect
and its riotous beauty.

you cup your hands
around my face
tilt my eyes toward the sun
and ask me what I want

another glass of wine
more menthol cigarettes
your tongue inside my vagina.

every small act
of rebellion we make
brings me closer
to forgetting

we only arrived here
on the backs of
our dead.

soon
it will be our turn
to die
and be
a place
lovers come
to shake off
their restless
histories.

32

don't think I don't know
that memory and longing
makes tourists of us.

don't imagine
I forget the spectacle
of humidity and place
and origin
and diaspora
and genocide
haunts us.

I know my place
is outside
this ravenous city

and you
are not a body
to claim as
admission.

I have been the ticket
to a foreign land,
fur bride
tranny
enough to know
all I want

is someone
who recalls
the deepest colour
of night is the almost blue
of morning.

33

the fluorescent blue of your eyeshadow
coils of nag champa
in the afternoon sunlight

an empty jug of water
by the bed

houseflies gathered
above the overflowing garbage bag
like a wreath of squirming flowers

your bare leg thrown over mine
the blush of my labia
against your outstretched hand

how heat travels through windows
wood
and lace

evening never comes here
though it is always just about to happen

the fourth of july parade
in the french quarter

a sea of tourists and locals
fireworks lit from the levee

a pile of rocks
called the end of the world

you flutter in front of me
riot of red floral prints
your headscarf trailing
behind you

each translucent image
leaves residue on my skin.

when they ask me what I know of joy
and ruin
I will not name a city
but a girl.

34

enough of desire's interrogation
give language
its weary absence
and say nothing.

you and I fell in love
in a distant summer
that won't return.

all the things I've loved
you
my dog
the scent of spring earth

outstrip their nomenclature.

better poets
make art
speak to entire histories
of violence.

I want none of it.

forget spillers
and simpson.

there is no greater theory
than the small wonder
of loving a woman
in a place entirely her own

each touch
each mouthful

a kinder text.

literature has nothing to teach me
I don't already know from your voice.

35

the night before I leave you
we slow dance
to billie holiday
on your kitchen floor

the flies lay maggots in the garbage bin

we sweep them up
in a frantic rush

the candles burn out
on your bedroom dresser

when night comes
we sleep nested against
the sky

my body
twice broken open
seeded with salt
and rust

grows something new
unnamed

made of gin, your scent and the blessed
weight of want.

36

we take no photographs
leave no record

no ledger
nor archive
to mark our place

only
two drunk girls
in the street

say nothing of splendour
or histories emerging
from our split tongues

once you said fucking me
felt too intimate
too close to bear

and I agreed
not knowing if I should say *I'm sorry*

or

you're welcome

if life wants something more of us
grander in design
world-breaking in our ontologies

make it
from handfuls of a night sky

new orleans

and mildewed sheets

everything beautiful in us
is already
dying.

"no
language is neutral seared into the spine's unravelling.
here is history too."

—Dionne Brand, *No Language Is Neutral*

37

what of history

or nation?

the text repairs itself
to meaning.

I am supposed to be weeping
in the pages.

instead I live.

38

high on cocaine
you spend hours between my thighs
rubbing my labia raw

I didn't know it could hurt
and feel good like this
until I met you

sometimes I orgasm
then close my legs around your head
trap you
demand more of your tongue
while you
breathless
and hungry

struggle to keep pace

later
I let you fuck me

not because I want it
but because it's expected of me
to trade pleasure
on rations

to sell my pussy back
manage your erection
as if it were
an obligation

sometimes
coming down on weed
and exhaustion

you tell me stories
of tehran

your boyhood
in another country
how the air smelled
what your mother wore in the morning

your grandfather, now dead
teaching you accounting
then revolution
uprising
your father imprisoned for years

until fleeing
to this snow-covered homeland

now you wait tables
do lines of coke
cut and ordered by a debit card

fuck a tranny
four times a week

this love
between us has an expiration date

I like the way
you wrap your arm around my waist

how you squeeze my hands in yours
and cradle my head against your chest

the soft ways
you buy my cunt

I lost my second virginity to you
though you don't know it

of course
we couldn't have lingered
in this exchange
we stretch it out
for five months

a trans woman
isn't worth much

my pussy too tight
laugh too deep

we make peace with our exiles

your home in two places
my body forever
in migration.

39

in montreal again
first time since surgery

I sit beside you in an anarchist café
with bad coffee.

the second woman
I've loved

it's an almost surprise
each time I want you

too new to this queer desire
to understand its rules.

once I said you had to get over
the idea of me.

loving a trans woman
is more about faith
than tolerance.

the ordinary wanting—
caffeine
your fingers along my bare arm
a new pair of jeans
fried chicken

in all the hours I spent
waiting in a hospital bed
or slipping into
an opioid sleep

I never imagined
such common lust

to be loved
for being difficult.

what am I now?

foundation on my cheeks
a maxipad in my purse

every ray of light

pierces me as if
I'm still
made of glass.

40

transsexuals die every day
but no one writes books about it.

I should account for the privilege
of being a learned tranny.

yes I have read your theory
though I prefer the poetics

I make with my body
between my legs,
on my knees.

which of these sins
should I answer for?

I let my hair grow long
and forget to shave my face.

something in my persistence
betrays my womanhood,

reveals me as pretender.
I don't blame you for looking for a more
coherent misery.

the only good trannies are already dead,

marsha p and miss rivera,
may they rest in power until

someone tweets their photographs,

twice yearly
when the cis perform allyship,
conjure our
digital beauty.

I apologize for not failing enough
to be worth saving,

for being raped
but not
beaten,
for writing another book

instead of disappearing.

41

what is poetry for
if not description?

I am never sure
when I've said enough
or need disclaimers.

imagine if language
failed us

and we spoke in gestures

instead of nouns?

without witness,
my body becomes
a field of crabapples,
split-red sour-sweet rotten.

here is a history
several of them
converge
in my mouth

like dandelion seeds
in April.

a country
claims me
without my consent.

I am a woman
until I'm not.

trans is not an identity

but a grave I rise from.

I indict my countries
for their crimes
first genocide
then apathy
I have no monument
big enough to hold my dead.
every day,
a new name blossoms.
this one shot
outside a bar
this one strangled
in her bed
this one stabbed 40 times
by her lover
this one beaten
by a pack of men

who to memorialize
and who to forget?

string a line of bodies
like a curtain around me,
hide my face
under murderous sky.

there is enough to live by

sometimes so much joy
it strips me bare

lilacs grow beside
the city asphalt
and
my mouth can't open
wide enough to sing
the possibility
still left in me.

I
am sometimes this,
suspected of being that,

derelict by night
abandoned by morning.

I never know when I blaze
or crouch,
when detail matters
or consumes.

I exceed
my language

I am more
than this white page

I craft a lodge here

like a lark nests
on a hydro pole,

precarious
and alien.

please

excuse my beauty.

I am

more or less
a poem,

an ndn,

a woman,

this language,
I break

the world
against.

42

weary of waiting
on miracles
on horoscopes
and tarot cards
on the chance for love
that never stops visiting
but refuses to live here.

I move past hope
into something fierce
and unyielding.
the graceless room
each solitary night
time spent lost
in redrafting
your voice
and the way

you cared for me.

I know my limit
by the careful way
cis people praise me.

my co-worker tells me
my breasts are bigger now
it's
compliment
and menace.

I want to die
but I don't.
there's a theory to my life
not written but felt.

in my dreams
I place my body in your bed
and never wake again.
stay with me

nurse my animal hurt.
let me leave the page
walk through your front door

pick lint from off your shoulder
linger in your kitchen
tag you on Insta.

be the ordinary intimacy

I always felt I was.

I went to the surgeon
thinking he would make you
love me
you don't
and never will.
how to live in my failure
to be a woman

walk through rain
my hair damp
and weightless

be in the world

without imagining
your face?

yes, I admit I lied

this body
knows nothing
I can call
a home.

Postscript

a question
of the text,
the title
and the footnote,[1]

each toward its end,
the place where language parts
from meaning

to emerge
at the breakwater

of what unmakes me.

if I've failed,
through artifice or image,
in conjure and by light,
let me apologize.

I only wanted to chase
the end of day

to the hem of night
and sit there
among the new stars
in a body of spun grass
until language
abandons me

and I turn back,
reluctant and confused,
to life.

1. I left every poem untitled to foreclose the possibility of loss, but still something is missing.

GWEN BENAWAY is a trans girl of Anishinaabe and Métis descent. She is the author of three previous collections of poetry—*Ceremonies for the Dead, Passage,* and *Holy Wild*, winner of the 2019 Governor General's Literary Award for Poetry. It was also a finalist for the Trillium Book Award for Poetry, the Lambda Literary Award for Transgender Poetry, and the Publishing Triangle Award for Trans and Gender-Variant Literature, and was longlisted for the Pat Lowther Memorial Award. She is the editor of an anthology of fantasy short stories titled *Maiden Mother and Crone: Fantastical Trans Femmes*. She has been a finalist for the Dayne Ogilvie Prize for LGBTQ Writers from the Writers' Trust of Canada, and her personal essay, "A Body Like A Home," was the Gold Prize Winner for the National Magazine Awards in Personal Journalism. She is also currently writing a new book of creative nonfiction, *trans girl in love. day/break* is her fourth book of poetry. She lives in Toronto, Ontario, and is a Ph.D. student at the University of Toronto in the Women and Gender Studies Institute.

Colophon

Manufactured as the first edition of
day/break
in the spring of 2020 by Book*hug Press

Edited for the press by Shane Rhodes
Copy edited by Stuart Ross
Cover design by Kate Hargreaves
Type by Jay Millar

bookhugpress.ca